Violoncello

WOLFGANG AMADEUS MOZART

CLARINET QUINTET
KLARINETTENQUINTETT

for Clarinet in A, 2 Violins, Viola and Violoncello
für Klarinette in A, 2 Violinen, Viola und Violoncello

A major / A-Dur
KV 581

Viola

CLARINET QUINTET

VIOLA

W. A. Mozart
K. 581

WOLFGANG AMADEUS MOZART

CLARINET QUINTET
KLARINETTENQUINTETT

for Clarinet in A, 2 Violins, Viola and Violoncello
für Klarinette in A, 2 Violinen, Viola und Violoncello

A major / A-Dur
KV 581

Clarinet in A

ALLE RECHTE VORBEHALTEN · ALL RIGHTS RESERVED

EDITION PETERS
LEIPZIG · LONDON · NEW YORK

CLARINET QUINTET

CLARINET in A

W. A. Mozart
K. 581

Clarinet in A

WOLFGANG AMADEUS MOZART

CLARINET QUINTET
KLARINETTENQUINTETT

for Clarinet in A, 2 Violins, Viola and Violoncello
für Klarinette in A, 2 Violinen, Viola und Violoncello

A major / A-Dur
KV 581

Violin I

ALLE RECHTE VORBEHALTEN · ALL RIGHTS RESERVED

EDITION PETERS
LEIPZIG · LONDON · NEW YORK

WOLFGANG AMADEUS MOZART

CLARINET QUINTET
KLARINETTENQUINTETT

for Clarinet in A, 2 Violins, Viola and Violoncello
für Klarinette in A, 2 Violinen, Viola und Violoncello

A major / A-Dur
KV 581

Violin II

ALLE RECHTE VORBEHALTEN · ALL RIGHTS RESERVED

EDITION PETERS
Leipzig · London · New York

CLARINET QUINTET

VIOLIN II

W. A. Mozart
K. 581

CLARINET QUINTET

VIOLONCELLO

W. A. Mozart
K. 581